THE DOMINION OF LIGHTS

THE DOMINION OF LIGHTS

Poems by

Isabel Nathaniel

Copper Beech Press

Providence

Grateful acknowledgment is made to the publications in which some of these poems first appeared: *Confrontation* ("The Paintings"), *Field* ("The Jewels of Windsor," "Miss Blue," "The Weepers"), *The Iowa Review* ("Two Gardenias in a Vase"), *The Journal* ("Intimate Possessions," "The Dominion of Lights," "Cartography," "The Grackles," "The Lake," "The Lake Revisited"), *The Nation* ("Galveston," "Elegy at Mustang Island," "Lost in the Forest near Nacogdoches," "The Garden"), *New Texas 91* ("The Ghosts of the Children"), *Ploughshares* ("The Coast of Texas"), *Poetry* ("Sick at the Gulf"), *Prairie Schooner* ("The Lie," "Afternoon," "The Visit," "Sunrise from the Seventh Floor"), *Southern Poetry Review* ("Peacocks"), and *The Texas Observer* ("The Boathouse," "On the Patio, Dallas").

Cover: René Magritte, *Empire of Light, II* (L'Empire des lumières, II), 1950. Oil on canvas, 31 x 39" (78.8 x 99.1 cm). The Museum of Modern Art, New York. Gift of D. and J. de Menil. Photograph ©1996 by the Museum of Modern Art, New York.

For information, address the publisher:
    Copper Beech Press
    English Department
    Box 1852
    Brown University
    Providence, Rhode Island 02912

Library of Congress Cataloging-in-Publication Data
Nathaniel, Isabel.
    The dominion of lights: poems / by Isabel Nathaniel.
        p.   cm.
    ISBN 0-914278-69-X (pbk. : alk. paper)
    I. Title.
PS3564.A8497D66   1996   96-3724
811'.54 — dc20   CIP

Set in Palatino by Louis Giardini
Printed and bound by McNaughton & Gunn
Manufactured in the United States of America
First Edition

for Bryan

for my sons
Christopher
and
Jerry John
(in memoriam)

CONTENTS

I

There are no fortunes to be told, although,
Because I love you more than I can say,
If I could tell you I would let you know.

W. H. Auden

LETTER

His love was in his word.
    I took his word to heart.
My heart was sepulcher,
    narrow house of dark.

His word lived in the dark
    and stunned my heart to live,
his exquisite mark
    sealed deep and secretive.

I bear his word-mark still,
    guerdon from that time
the heart adorned its cell
    with intricate design.

THE DOMINION OF LIGHTS

Magritte paints darkness on a row of houses,
yet the sky is blue and midday bright.
Night is on the street, the lamps are lit,
the trees are black, the chimneys profiled black
against the contradiction: sky
so absolutely of the day. And I

almost see the same capriccio
there across the museum garden, there
on Fifty-fourth Street where dark has gathered
strangely on the row of houses, tricking
memory, as if I lived there once,
as if I'd lit the lamp in afternoon.

See that window, draperies drawn back,
lampshade glowing gold on the familiar:
brass, mahogany, linen, velvet,
table, sofa, bookcase, clock (yet no one
moves behind the window, no illuminated
figures framed in darkness, no evidence

of lives in motion, no woman reading
in the parlor, no two small boys at play
around her). In the right imagination
she looks up (the light gone bad? a shadowing?)
and reaches with an ease, reaches past
the vase of (tulips?) and switches on the lamp.

Magritte is painting version after version,
ten versions. Night is always on the houses.
Sky is always aqua-blue and bright.
The lamps are lit. Is it afternoon?
The scene is heightened by the lack of motion.
(Where are the boys, their perfect quickness?)

One early April afternoon I waited,
facing the glass overlooking the garden,
the plots of ivy blackish-green of winter,
the birches filming in new green.
I would not have thought especially
of darkness, my boys were young. I waited merely

noticing the details of the garden,
the somber ivy, the birches (newly planted?)
noticing across on Fifty-fourth Street
a window, draperies drawn back, a lamp
lighted in the afternoon, tulips,
a woman, two small boys, that moment.

TERRACE AT SAINTE-ADRESSE

1866

The summerday light
flattens, so that all
appears closer than normal
and the colors are pushed
past what they are.

The man and the woman
are as never afterward.
The whipping of the flags
the red of the poppies
has just happened.

And the voices
are soft by the water
unhurried
as the distance takes color,
pressed forward by the wind.

THE PAINTINGS

Renoir—Dancing at the Moulin de la Galette

We are in love, center left. You
are wearing top hat, I'm in white.
How close your arms pull me, your hands
on my ass. You're drunk and telling
outrageous things and kissing my ear.
Why did you always say you couldn't dance?
Isn't it grand in the sun?
I have nothing on under my white dress.
I can feel your erection perfectly.

Boudin—Lunch in a Garden

Not the couple in the foreground,
but seated behind red roses
nearly under the trees, talking
intently. So seriously. Philosophy,
I think. Why is the man, brown hat
in his hand, looking at us? I'll have
more wine. Lunch in a garden.
Two glasses of wine and I'll say I
love you.

Renoir—The Luncheon of the Boating Party

Upper right corner, almost
out of the picture. Not dressed
for boating like the others—
my black gloves, silk elegance.
Those in the party grow blowsy with sun and wine.

How they lean into the golden day!
It is easy. They make it look easy
and as if there is no hurry.
You stand, opposite, considering all that I will be
for you. You are staunch with hope.
Can you make out the figure behind me?—
as if given form, then obscured by cropping.
Look now—his hat, part of his face,
trouser leg and shoe, his hand
about my waist. Barring such scrutiny
we might think ourselves amongst the revelers,
slurred and sweet in pleasure.

THE BOATHOUSE

You come as the dead come, poised
in the quiet, offering up again
pines, stairs to the lake.
Places where you were. Now my mind

holds you, completes you, steers
you in the story: here is a boathouse
like the one of our childhood. Within
the light is tremulous and green,

possessed by the lakewater, obedient
to its rhythms. The boat, helpless,
is rocked by its own image.
At first we intrude, stand clear,

but the rippled glare claims
us, arranges us in old gestures.
Enclosed in its secrets, we breathe
in time to the motion on the walls.

THE INCLINE

He descended
singing, his hair immensely red
in the full-green end of summer
the trees thickening closed
the air breath-temperature and sweet.
From the higher road he passed
through sheets of sunlight, the bay
rising strong against the drop.

Down farther was the weed grass
still as if with thunder coming
the season held this side of dying.
And come from the shore way
the woman walked,
her legs wet and her white dress
dark where the water had leaped.

TWO GARDENIAS IN A VASE

The scent is everywhere, a slow weight
of sweetness. Languor at first
that hangs in the quiet of this room.
Now, soon, the sweetness is your own breath
until you can imagine the heroines
of Late Movies and Bette Davis
sends the letter to Mr. Hammond.
I absolutely must see you,
come at eleven. Smooth white blooming
in a crystal vase brought from England
to Singapore. Bette Davis works her lace
and waits. He's been her lover
for years. The perfume in the room
is a frenzy now. He prefers
the Asian woman who powders her face
to a mask and wears gold chains.
The gardenias go too far, deep curl
of the petals, a drug of scent
like making love. Later she lies
about why she killed Mr. Hammond.
She has fired six times in all.

THE LIE

Quick and graceful,
it glides past
(as it is meant to do)

and only later
does some small fault
begin to flutter,
a pale fascination,
until there's no help
but to call it back:

impeccably arranged,
delicately embellished,
but darkening somewhat
and unraveling.

It is a lie

trapped word by word
over and over,
the deceived and the lie
coupled in the room,
at each other all day,
grown frowsy and desperate

for release,
for what comes next,
the liar's return, the face
that brazens it out,
insists, protests,

admits, the mouth already fixed
in complaint *trust me, trust me.*

CARTOGRAPHY

1.

These maps are early,
inaccurate. I cannot gauge
distances we keep. Named places

are not there. Find me.
Summer has already started.
I waste my days like money.

2.

Suppose in arbitrary cities
it is spring. Mild suns
shine what we wished for.

We contrive to touch
fingers, hair. In strange rooms
I untie my blouse.

3.

Manhattan sky in strips
is innocently blue. Halfway between
rivers I could show you gulls.

Irish setters, Labradors
swim Castle Lake in Central Park,
shake collar-tags like bells.

By now you're gone for good
from a somnolent, red-brick town.

You're three days farther west
in a city of horizons.
Lives don't break free.
Where can we wake up making love?

4.

Describe the color
I have forgotten the color
of your eyes, she wrote.
Forgot the color of the overcoat he wore
in Union Station,
knew the precise feel
her hands down his spine. In strange rooms
untied her blouse.

She walks river to river in her city
as if she were on to something
surprising. Softness unaccountably
under her feet.

Take off your clothes, he said.
She untied her blouse. Eyes
blue or grey.

5.

Bad days the sky is a vague smoke
lowering. There's no place
where the sun's coming from.

What were we going to do? who
did I think I was?
Nevertheless

as in a movie I am
crossing bright piazzas
towards you where you must be

or arriving
at capital city airports
our lives about to begin.

6.

I received your letter of June 15
written 1:20 a.m. lying naked and
drunk, motel on a ten-lane expressway,

just to let me know you
love me and wish I were with you.

7.

Pedestrian en route, block
by block something surprising.
Florist bouquets mark murder sites.
Carnations, baby's breath and freesia
acknowledge the fallen. She elaborates her city.
Bannisters are brass, morning glories
twist up string in windows.
The break in traffic
is a kind of listening.

AUBADE AT THE ALGONQUIN

Rumbles in the closet wall
grow benevolent, familiar. Day
never seeks our airshaft window.
I must touch you awake
unhurried as first light.

Watch me a while—at ease
kissing your shoulders. This is
the third morning. Move
your mouth against my breast.
It's almost noon. Cock crow.

AFTERNOON

High-up rooms, much light, air, and polished
floors, plants healthy as banyan trees
in the sun. The cat in the best sun.
You in the sun, *your* desk with the river view, tugboats
and barges, a zippy sailboat. Certainly gulls.
I've been someplace, I come home, I'm
slightly out of breath with a good day.
I walked twenty blocks. Listened to
a music student play Brahms on a big xylophone
at 59th and 5th. The traffic ruined the soft notes
but the crowd was hushed and clapped hard
when he finished. We are drinking wine now
and I am telling you about it. Look
how the river throws the light back.

THE GHOSTS OF THE CHILDREN

Goodbye, goodbye, everybody said
at the airport, but the ghosts
of the children have not gone
to their *real* houses. All week
they are here, best behaved,
fluent and withdrawing like fishes
through the white silence.
The ghosts of the children play
long beyond visitation rights

a comfort, carefully at a distance,
smooth and mild in the spaces
which keep them. In your own breath
you hear their language room to room
until finally in the evenings
their names will not answer
and you look for them, but
the cool arcs where they trespassed
fill in.

BLACK COATS

1.

After a long night of snow he cleans the glass,
considers the light, while the people of the city
in black coats and galoshes keep moving.

I have booked a room in the Grand Hôtel de Russie.
I have begun my series of Boulevards. Pissarro's
working at the window: carriages' dark to and fro,
pedestrians' intricate crisscross. Parisians
advancing from here to there.

On the way to love or money in long black coats,
immaculately tailored, they spill, they surge
so that even the befuddled, the distraught, the mad
are swept along and it is hard to distinguish
in this *trottoir* crowd, those whose fever
is excessive, their faces flushed in the white air,
those whose black coats are whichway
and who have forgotten to put on their galoshes.
They are out walking, walking with everyone else
because it feels like going somewhere, soggy feet
leaving traces on solid ground.

2.

What I consider first is atmosphere and effect.
I see only patches of color, accord of tones.

In black the crowds are going somewhere,
blurred by light. In this atmosphere
the distraught, the mad, the merely befuddled
are making headway. Is it possible
to crisscross to love or money? Her face

is flushed, she has lost her gloves.
The great problem is to bring tiniest details
within the harmony of the whole. Meticulous,
he scrapes his palette, squeezes color,
the silver-white which is light.

There was a time she owned a dozen pairs
of gloves. Her love, her money and her looks
are gone. He strokes her in, blurred black.
Le Boulevard Montmartre, C. Pissarro '97.

THE JEWELS OF WINDSOR

Sotheby exhibit and sale, Geneva

Back from a frenzy of glory in war,
modern in bold check and floppy tie,
he favors his left profile.
Prince of Promise, hails the populace
but George V still thinks his fidget son
poor David—small and pretty crybaby
with Victoria's hollowed eyes.
My father doesn't like me,
the prince glooms over brandy.
And mother Mary's German chill
curves back to childhood,
endless white slide of ice.

Drowning now in Wallis, hidden
and found, he heaps his love's
lean bosom with jewels,
sends schoolboy *billets-doux:*
"A boy is holding so very very
tight. More and more and more."
Papa dead, we know poor David's story.
Here are the years precise
in jewels. Gorgeous plethora—
diamonds, rubies, David's penance
(he had not made things right)
the Alexandra emeralds, pearls
(he had not made things right)
sapphires to bring out her eyes,
menagerie of Cartier beasts,
the panther crouches on 90 carats,
the blazing leopard stalks her wrist.
My Wallis from her David.
Hold tight. More and more and more.

INTIMATE POSSESSIONS

Jack London Ranch, Glen Ellen, California, 1948

I warn you I dislike biographers
but come in, come in. Let's forego
preliminary chatter. You shall see directly
what you have journeyed six thousand miles to see,
the artifacts you think you need for truth.
I agreed to that. This way. Let me take your arm—

How your letter surprised me! While so many make
the pilgrimage to my Jack, you're first to look
for Robert Louis Stevenson in my house.
What a relentless breed biographers are,
following a scent, like that Stone fellow
who betrayed me—but here we are, behold!—

the R.L.S. china, our luncheon to be served
upon it. You look about to faint, sit down.
Did you expect your holy relics wrapped
in cellophane? I assure you these plates and cups
will last another meal. Best pour some wine,
our local Chardonnay. A pity the goblet

was not also your Great Man's, but sacramental,
all the same, in that Jack held it (surprising smallness
of his hands, taper fingers) to toast
(mellifluous, whispering voice) the life and work
of your Louis. Ah, you have a lovely smile.
You've recovered. Now Chan will ladle pumpkin soup

into a piece of precious Stevensoniana. I tease,
but I do not underestimate the power
of intimate possessions. Facts alone
reveal nothing, however careful your notes
(chinaware white, green-and-tan-lined border,
manufactured 1875 by Hubbe).

When you are back in Edinburgh some small
feeling of Louis's soup bowl will persist,
intensify—but of course you know that,
you are already living *in* the man.
I can relax that it's not Jack you steal
from me. Now, salmon from our Pacific—

delicious, but chosen with deliberation
(as was the pumpkin soup) for color,
to complement the pretty trim of the plate.
Yes, I have a good eye. See how my tiles
and walls repeat the peacock green. I remember
this shade on woodwork at Vailima.

On horses we rode the miles up the rank slope
from Apia. The house was closed but we pressed
our foreheads against each window to peek.
Then we hiked the clogged switchback trail to the summit.
It was late in the day and the jungle heat was suffocating.
"I wouldn't have gone out of my way to visit

the grave of any other man in the world,"
Jack said. Before the *Snark* hoisted anchor
he held like charms, these pieces, these reliquiae,
these plates, these cups his idol's hands
and lips had touched. (Mate, Mate,
the short life of Louis was longer than your own!)

Coffee? Dessert? Chan has created something
perfect with mangoes, I believe.
Do describe Vailima now and the months
you were privileged to live there. Did you sense
. . . morbid qualities? Our visit, of course,
was long ago when Samoans told tales

of the site as an ancient fort, a bloody
battlefield haunted by ghosts of the slain—
superstition or the supernatural?
How will you tell it? (growth, undergrowth tangled,
trees groping for light, dangled ropes
of liana). How will you explain

what is real on the islands? (violence of colors,
the red frangipani, hibiscus; orchids
like cancers wild in the branches). Our descent
from the summit seemed harder than the climb.
It was too late in the day, toward evening.
The trees met overhead, the bush closed in.

An ancient war had been fought on *Tusitala's* land.
Oh the hush of the place, something waiting.
Jack led the way, darkness was falling,
phosphor of decaying wood shone
under our feet. My mind is no less exotic
than Samoans'—what they said was there,

was there. I name it in their word, *aitu*.
It did not clutch, but lightly caressed Jack's shoulder.
—Is this how I should tell it? To look back
I use my inward eye, seeing to where
truth is elaboration, each glimmering
detail something more. It is consolation

to sit here amongst the curios (shells,
corals, dancing sticks, calabashes,
porpoise teeth, anklets, armlets, skirts
of human hair), the windows' watery light
surprisingly abundant, when outside
all is shrouded by redwood and madrone.

Upon my death no one is to live here
nor change my arrangements of intimate possessions.
Here the relic china belongs, displayed
with true affection—because a dreaming boy
sailed to the rim when he crammed his head
with R.L.S. at Oakland Public Library

and boy (with his books) sails on the *Snark*
and reads aloud on deck: *I travel not*
to go anywhere, but to go (ubiquitous
safety-match bookmarks falling), *I saw that island*
first when it was neither night nor morning.
We are listening—Nakata the cabin boy,

Wada the cook, Captain Warren, Martin,
Hermann and I—of course we're all of roving
disposition, these are our happiest days. . . .
How my memory shifts direction (an adventure,
an art) but I see you are near anxiety
that I am lost and you are stuck

on the littered deck: bunches of bananas,
coconuts, baskets of yams, oranges, taro,
pumpkins, bound and protesting chickens, a piglet
and a little decorated papaya tree
set in a kerosene can. Yes, well,
I know I claimed some calm or horror at

Vailima, *which* I cannot be sure.
Never mind, you are headed for Silverado
(an hour's drive and a stiff climb) to play out
Louis's squatter honeymoon: abandoned
silvermine downfalling, wreck and rust,
parlor of poison oak and whizzing rattlesnakes,

oh your rash, hemorrhagic Scot and his
American bedlamite, marriage *in extremis!*
(He did love her, she did love him.)
Will you write against brave Fanny Stevenson
(as that Stone fellow wrote against me), set down
that a Great Man married the wrong woman? How

will you tell it? The *real* in exotic latitude.

II

It is better to go to the house of mourning
than to go to the house of feasting;
for this is the end of everyone,
and the living will lay it to heart.

Ecclesiastes

THE VISIT

In the kitchen I tell your mother and grandmother,
don't worry. They are polite
but concerned. I want to be shown
how to make white gravy and biscuits.
They think you're a fool, marrying
again. They are sorry I'm from New York.
This sky is different, like a foreign country,
like Russia. I could know it from Chekhov.
There could be two rows of tall, closely planted
trees, like walls, forming an avenue. Tomorrow
I'll meet your brothers and sisters.
Your sons will arrive, and smile at me.
In the evening the band will play in the plaza.
Here the trees would be live oak, green all year.

ON THE PATIO, DALLAS

The prickly pear and yucca
dug from a roadside
do fine in pots. Sun,
sunflowers. The August heat.
Petunias, pinks, and even the geranium
probably don't belong. With watering
they hold on. One morning
I fed them Ortho Fertilizer
made entirely of sea-going fish.
I hosed the place till
the hanging baskets dripped
and the fence soaked dark.
There rose the brackish
smell of bays and wharves
and I turned my head
to the distance as if to hear
the regular slapping of the sea.

THE GRACKLES

Seven boat-tailed grackles rule
back here at poolside, fanatical
as Furies, all black swoop and curse.
From green circumference of palms
they whistle reckoning, penalty,
ride downdrafts of turquoise air
to eye you. What have you done?
Again and again their long beaks part
to tell you it's irrevocable, voices
wired for thrill, for special effects.

We feign insouciance, stretched
and heat-stunned on our little claims,
chaises longues. Even the luckiest
behind closed eyelids dreams a different
choice, wakes and hears the rasp
of palm blades, knows he's got it coming.

PEACOCKS

In the dark they are screaming
exquisite messages—a chorus
of crazies in brilliant high-pitch.

Unseen in the black trees, each
in its own madness calls *may-awe,*
may-awe: something fervent and extreme.

The sky over Bandera, Texas, is sky
its true color, stars before
they got tired. Tonight is like

the ancient world, flat and trembling,
and this its lavish hour
of bad news. The beaked crone

inside your head could screech
these omens, these monotones
of regret: ships afire, kings

undone, wrongheaded heroes broken,
dragged, *may-awe, may-awe.*
From the far side of your brain

you'll shrill such voice someday
under a city's diminished stars—
a blackened bag-lady all night awake

in a delirium of whatever happened.

MISS BLUE

Hattie's Place, a brothel operating 1896-1946 in San Angelo, Texas, was sealed shut by Texas Rangers. It is now open as a museum.

Thirteen steps, a landing, thirteen more
rise to old lust—second story rooms
in a rage of Texas June heat.
This is authentic. Haven't you always
been curious? A thumbtacked *Ring Bell For Service*
is the last madam's surviving scribble.

Velvet and gilt in the front parlors try
at grand decadence, but this was never
New Orleans, never Chicago. This was always
too many slow hard miles from anywhere.
The players here were cowboys and soldiers
out all day with the lizards in 109°, insane
metallic chirr of cicadas a refrain in their heads.

Here are the cribs, these hold the evidence,
the mysteries. Ten little sanctums with screendoors.
Five opposite five. The long, dark and thrilling
hall between them. The screendoors hardly censor,
hinging open, clapping close, incongruous
backporch sound in this corridor resounding,
surely, with melodrama acted on the iron beds.

There was always one called Miss Blue in #5
distinguished by indigo motif, tinted light bulb,
and something more—a peephole. A spy's eye
on the other side ogles in your mind
until you are sentient of yourself, bathed blue
and ghostly in the tilted dressing table mirror
and you see it is possible to fall in love

with your own allure. If bad luck, steelblue spike,
had driven you to this feverish godforsaken room,
back then, you'd keep your insolent eyes
on your own silverblue reflection
shining there where it's winter,
where the cold white ground is blue.

SICK AT THE GULF

Poisoned perhaps. Last night's catch-of-the-day
with sauce Béarnaise. Or imagine something worse—
those plagues transmitted by intermediary host.

It's possible. We traipsed every slough, ridge
and flat of the wildlife refuge. Mosquitoes.
Surely fleas and ticks. You suggest *just a virus*

and with Pepto-Bismol, alarm dissipates
into a fevered hush. Immobilized, propped
on condo terrace, I look to sea in mild pathos

and think Chekhovian: stricken heroine
sent to the Crimea's sunny winter
for her health. Unhappy exile in Yalta's

lush heat, cypresses, palms—but snow
enters her dreams, white grounds,
white roofs, birches white with rime.

Feeling better? is your offered optimism,
along with an icy drink, but her answer
is falling away and you cannot hear

her wish to return to the capital
where she has many admirers.
In grief and ecstasy she burns
like a reckless comet, unlucky and luminous.

GALVESTON

We keep the shutters drawn all afternoon
against the sun. It's the custom here.
Light filters through, wavery as water.
The sun's the enemy to beat. We trust
the seawall to hold the gulf, but drowning
is our fate. Be careful on these stairs.

I must catch my breath. It's the steep stairs
and the heat. I lie down in the afternoon,
the quiet so close it feels like drowning.
This climate robs all strength if you stay here
too long. When I arrived I was a trust-
ing girl whose only fear was the water.

That's your room, rose-papered and a water
view. How young you are to take the stairs
two at a time! You'll visit me, I trust,
in my room across the hall. Each afternoon
I rest from three to five. It's not uncommon here
to find solace in a dim room, drowning

until dinnertime. Of course the drownings
no one forgets were long ago. Water
swept the city down. Six thousand died here,
their bodies stacked high as stairs
and burned. The foul smoke turned afternoon
dark. To rebuild after that was a trust.

I've picked gardenias for your bedside. Don't trust
their scent. Breathed close, you will be drowning
in languor. A trap set to steal your afternoon.
Would you like refreshments? Rosewater,
perhaps, or wine? There's no one on the stairs.
Brandy, chocolates? We're quite sequestered here,

our rooms a refuge from the crowds here
in high summer. Port cities can't be trusted.
In this fancy street more than one stair
led to a brothel, nomad sailors drowning
in unimagined pleasures and watered-
down liquor. But this is *our* afternoon.

Here is your treat. Brandy in the afternoon.
You trusted our complicity on the stairs.
In this watery light we lie down as if drowned.

THE COAST OF TEXAS

If it's appendicitis, you're in trouble
out here on the *Isla de Malhado*.
Despite bright stars there are disturbances.
It's three o'clock in the morning.

Ashore on the *Isla de Malhado*
the shipwrecked Spanish came to no good end.
It's three o'clock in the morning.
If it's not an emergency, go back to bed.

The shipwrecked Spanish come to a bad end,
lost and unlucky in the New World.
If it's not an emergency, go back to bed.
The balcony is drifting out to sea.

You're lost and unlucky in a new world,
four hours till it lightens to a morning.
The balcony is drifting out to sea.
You heard a bosun's pipe above the tide.

For hours it is lightening to morning.
The pain on your right side is a warning
as was the bosun's pipe above the tide.
Your nightgown is white batiste and lace.

The pain on your right side is warning,
and the red aureole around the moon.
Your nightgown of white batiste and lace
is in reckless windborne flight

toward a red aureole around the moon.
The wretched Spanish huddled on the beach,
their barge in windborne flight
toward still further shores of darkness.

THE WEEPERS

In 1528 the shipwrecked Cabeza de Vaca and a dwindling number of armada survivors lived for a time with Indians who roamed the narrow islands of the Texas coast. His account describes their curious ritual of weeping, how as another culture might salute or bow or make the sign of the cross, these people wept.

This is the island named Misfortune
where Karankawas are weeping
and the sea is wildly in agreement:
sorrow, sorrow.
           From the terrace
how white everything white is in the dark,
simplified and heightened:
parallel lines of waves fixed
as if by brush in titanium white
and the beach a long white stroke
to darkness.
           It would be the same
even then, this edge of the New World.
This sea over and over, this trek of moon.
The wind in this direction,
this smell of salt, of weather.
           And the weepers
starting up. A half hour of wails
for greeting. How are you? Not too good.
Simplified and heightened.
The castaways were impressed
with such lively sense of their own calamity.
To this island we gave the name Malhado.

Night makes dark mirrors of the terrace windows.
Inside I appear out there, come
so far, castaway from some
           old world.

The weepers are assembled, their lamentation
rising in this direction, profound, insistent,
all the years ahead
come to an end alike forlorn and fatal.

THE LAKE

At first I would go that far
to the place you prefer,
shadow-black landscape,
brink of the lake,
then out to the profound center,
drowning down to enter
the place you prefer.

Thus you could not help
but love me, a griever
dressed in white and come that far.
Remember? I lit candles,
splendor for your sunless state of mind.

Illuminated all around us
were your perfect sorrows—
each a boy-child, earnest
and polite in a southern way.
"Don't cry, I love you,"
I called to one or the other
and reached out my arms
to sorrows, as might a good mother.

And always there was recurring
in some impenetrable tangle
outside the light—the father—
disturbing and significant as a riddle.
Remember? I chanted answers,
rapture trilling in my throat.

Catacomb of extravagant melancholy—
I would go that far.
My arrogant imperative
was to redeem the haunted boy-child's

losses, to purify the father
into what he'd never been.

How could you not
love me—white priestess
of exquisite possibilities.
Remember? I went by touch,
magic shivering in my hand.

THE LAKE REVISITED

Our guide has taken us this far,
his pontoon boat a desecrating
roar on somber Caddo Lake.
You and I play tourists,
though these infernal regions
I know by heart.

Calmly middle-aged we sit, apart,
and stare at cypress rising
thick and dark out of this labyrinth
of twisting river off its course.

There is no outside world.
Sloughs and bayous snake and narrow
among brakes of cypress
and grey festoons of Spanish moss
curtain out all distance.
I need no guide.

It is underworld. The moss sways
graceful and furtive, like old selves.
No parasite, it feeds on dust and rain
and so grows slowly—away from the future.
Each tiny plant in the contorted garland
bears one yellow flower in the spring—
small spirits suspended.

Our guide has cut the motor for effect:
the silence of the dead
into which the crow, the heron
are not afraid to call.
Even as I called in those days
for effect, not believing in death,
not knowing death shadowed my son.

The stilled boat rests on a version of itself
that won't be still. With expertise
it undulates its way and takes us,
like tourists wanting their money's worth,
deeper for effect, bending, cavorting
among the mirrored darks, the greys,
the little yellows.

ELEGY AT MUSTANG ISLAND

The Mayan Princess fronts the Gulf,
crescent of white stucco.
Its surprise, its excess—
for this wind-blown barrier island—
is an extravaganza of pools and gardens,
pinks of perfumed blooms, jungly greens,
all vigilantly tended
to thrive so in the hunkered-down space
between hotel and ridge of dunes.

April weather chancy, the place
is all ours. We're warmed,
lulled in man-made Eden.
The sea we came for is just over there,
surf-sound close, continuous.
On white chaises longues we lie
in an attitude of mild happiness
and find amusement in gulls'
periodic fracas overhead.

For passion we substitute politeness.
Our paradise was more than this,
once, but a swift strike of the gods
has rendered us quiet and untroublesome.
There's a way out: a boardwalk
snakes over sand little-Sierras
and a door alone against the sky
guards the ramp's descent to beach.
Arm in arm, we've been out there

for dutiful strolls, our delicate feet
just managing not to touch
blue-neon *physalia physalis,*
those man-of-war hellions delivered onto shore,

tendrils still armed to sting
into agony. We step right along
taking menace for granted.
For us the tideline's runes
spell out tragedy already happened.

My tragedy that happened
is always there, dark
as the west side of the dunes
in this early-morning, low-angled light.
Sea oats, dove weeds, pennyworts,
goatsfoot morning glory
make the rich mat of vegetation
that traps the sand. These plants,
like a long-there grief,

lie half buried, roots and runners spreading,
sprouting blooms at night
to know full beauty at the dawn.
I make the ascent. Last day, there is some calm
or horror yet to be identified.
Grey veils of air are walls and ceiling
for the boardwalk door which opens
hard against the southeast wind.
From here it is possible to call

long sing-song sounds, the way
kids call—and I send out in graceful glide
my dead son's name in syllables: *Jer-ry* . . .
Jer-ry . . . *Jer-ry* . . . his name offered to him.
And that most important word
skips naturally and unimpeded
across the ghostly beach,
over the silvering water,
past the horizon of oil-rigs

and out there joins him,
my boy, O so wholly himself
this brief morning moment,
because his own name is far sweeter
than silence, his own name
rising and falling in the air,
a music he has missed,
his name *Jer-ry . . . Jer-ry . . . Jer-ry . . .*
coming to him.

SUNRISE FROM THE SEVENTH FLOOR

What a view—it's theater from up here.
As night thins away, the play begins.
Every morning I've watched, my ritual,
to be seated on the terrace in time
for the pageant. Think of the beach
as stage, bare and blackened, but light

from the scrim of sky seeps, palely lights
a figure crossing downstage center. Here
the scarfed lady makes her beach
appearance, ghostly, to begin
a graceful climb of boardwalk. Timing
is perfect—she'll complete the ritual

of wiping tar from feet, observe the ritual
of sunrise and head on in for a light
breakfast in the lounge. I wonder what time
she gets up, for godsake! I'm out here
by six. And the bearded man begins
his swim about now, just as the beach

blazes in red. His dogs hit the beach
first, we all have our little rituals.
A sea-god, all forte, he begins
stroking the crimson swath of waterlight
that ends in oil rigs, offshore monuments here
at the Gulf, black stonehenges for our time.

To the kitchen for more coffee, just time
enough to lose both deity and his beach
pups. Binoculars find instead what's common here—
laughing gulls joined in group ritual,
lined up squadron facing the wind, not light,
synchronized and ready to begin

what motions of the air command. Begin!
I think my dead son's name. And summertimes
when only specks of sorrow touched us lightly.
Zephyr, direct the boy and me back to a beach
we knew. Nothing bad can happen. Let ritual
keep them by monotonous waves. Hear

the mother call each time, *come here,*
come here. He begins to run across the beach.
The light will set and rise and set, a ritual.

LOST IN THE FOREST NEAR NACOGDOCHES

You're leading the way and I am sighing
behind you. At each wrong turn the dogs
patiently hesitate and I am sighing.
So wait here and rest you say, in charge,
as though you were a huntsman
dressed in coarse brown cloth,
as though you knew the way out

and I am waiting, kept
in a childhood tale of forest
where this is routine and believable:
the perilous path, repeated adversity.
I wait, enclosed by courtly pines
and silence, the dutiful dogs gone on,
imprinted to your shape of the huntsman.

Now all that moves is alive.
Leaf by leaf stirs from its branch
and issues language in its slow drift down
and the wind collaborates to make
a chorus, prompting. I have only to listen
for the one correct word, the word
most hidden and most familiar,

as watery November sun asserts itself
to light at my feet a highway of ants
who know exactly where they are going.
Each parading forager carries a berry
of ecstatic fuchsia hue, a splendor
astonishing on the brown mulched floor.
Little pilgrims, little caravan of the faithful,

I would join in this ancient choreography
and carry a bright precious fruit
as votive offering to reclaim the favor

of heaven. For leaf after leaf
is saying the word *loss, loss*
and the wind is the moan of grieving.
We are lost in the forest near Nacogdoches

and you and the dogs are trying
to look cheerful as you return to me.
Faithful huntsman, there is a way
out of here, we are walking
the procession of centuries and I am holding
a branch heavy with clustered berries
of reddish purple which shine

with an aura. Are they not like
sorrows we have accumulated
in this life, each a luminary
which we must carry with us
more carefully than a guerdon,
more carefully than a piece of luck?

THE GARDEN

A place like a painting. Think of
the garden of Monet. No problems
but those the brush can handle.
Let's live here: profuse dahlias
and me in white dress with blue sash.
Our sons, animated by the trick of light,
concern themselves with hoops
and little wooden horses. The incandescence
burns features away and loss
is unpredictable.

In the pleasure of reds and greens
we wait. Your summer straw and linen
are swirls and dabs. Your face
has no layering of memory.
We live here, the garden table is set
for tea. These are our figures
dazzled in such light as though
afternoon were our favorite time
and we had not yet been cruel
to one another.